The Crocodile and the Plover

Written by Kerrie Shanahan

Illustrated by Omar Aranda

Flying Start
to Literacy®

Contents

Chapter 1:

An egg all alone

Many years ago, there was a mother crocodile. She watched her nest, day and night, keeping her eggs safe from animals that wanted to eat them.

One hot day, she went to the river. While she was gone, a lizard crept towards the nest.

Suddenly, the crocodile burst out of the water. She chased the lizard. Her strong jaws were open wide and her sharp teeth were gleaming. *Snap!*

The lucky lizard escaped. The crocodile's eggs were safe in their nest . . . all except for one!

This one egg rolled all the way to the edge of the river. The egg lay on the edge of the river all by itself.

Nearby, a plover watched the egg.

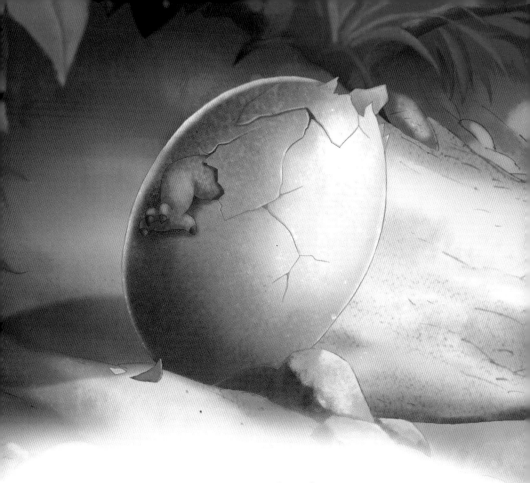

A noise came from inside the egg.

Peep! Peep! Peep!

Inside the egg, a baby crocodile pecked
at the hard shell with her egg tooth.
Finally, the shell cracked and the crocodile
hatched.

The plover watched as the baby crocodile pushed its way out of the egg.

She was sad that the baby crocodile was alone. She flew over to the crocodile and showed her how to catch insects and how to drink water from the river.

Chapter 2:
A new friendship

As the months went by, the plover and the crocodile became good friends. They spent all their time together, playing in the river and catching insects to eat.

After some time, the crocodile wanted to hunt other animals to eat. It was time for her to explore the river, build her own nest and become a mother.

And it was time for the plover to leave the river and build a nest. The crocodile and the plover said goodbye.

Chapter 3:

A new life

Years passed.

The crocodile made nests, laid her eggs and looked after her baby crocodiles. She had to protect her eggs and baby crocodiles from the animals that wanted to eat them.

Up and down the river, all the other animals were scared of the crocodile because she was a strong and powerful hunter.

The plover also laid eggs and raised her young. She often thought about her friend and wondered what she was doing now.

Then, one year, there was very little rain.
This dry year was followed by another
dry year, and another.

It was a drought. The water in the river
almost dried up.

It was a hard time for the plover.
It was dangerous for her to drink at the river
where the hungry crocodiles were waiting
for an animal to eat.

But she had to do it. She ran swiftly
and drank.

As the drought continued, the plover became weaker and slower. She still went to the river to drink, but it was now very dangerous.

One day, as she bent to sip the water, an enormous crocodile jumped out of the river.

The plover froze, closed her eyes and waited.

But the crocodile's sharp teeth didn't grab
her and the crocodile's jaws didn't snap shut!

The plover opened her eyes.
There was her friend from many years ago.

Chapter 4:

Old friends

The crocodile saw that her old friend, the plover, was weak and starving. Slowly, she opened her large mouth. The plover stepped away in fear, but the crocodile told her to come closer.

The plover looked inside her old friend's
mouth.   She could see pieces of food stuck
in between the crocodile's teeth.

There, inside the crocodile's mouth was
a meal, and the plover was very, very
hungry.   The plover didn't know what to do.
Could it be a trick?

The plover pecked a piece of food out of the crocodile's teeth. The crocodile didn't move. Again, the plover pecked a piece of food from her old friend's teeth.

Peck! Peck! Peck!

The plover had a wonderful meal. She was
very happy. And the crocodile was very
happy, too, because now her teeth were nice
and clean.

The plover and the crocodile were happy together at the edge of the river . . . just as they had been when they were young.

And, to this day, crocodiles and plovers live happily together on the edge of rivers.

A note from the author

While I was researching a non-fiction book about crocodiles, I found out that a bird called the Egyptian plover lives side-by-side with the Nile crocodile. For thousands of years, people have believed that these two animals have a special relationship where the plovers pick out leftover meat from in-between the crocodiles' teeth. This helps the crocodiles because it stops germs from rotting their teeth. And because it helps the crocodiles, they don't eat the plovers.

But scientists have no proof that this special relationship exists. It is a myth! This made me think: how did such a myth begin? And that's how I came to write this traditional tale.